The Medieval Islamic World

Conflict and Conquest

Jessica Cohn, M.S.

Publishing Credits

Dona Herweck Rice, *Editor-in-Chief*
Lee Aucoin, *Creative Director*
Torrey Maloof, *Editor*
Neri Garcia, *Senior Designer*
Stephanie Reid, *Photo Researcher*
Rachelle Cracchiolo, M.S.Ed., *Publisher*

Teacher Created Materials

5301 Oceanus Drive
Huntington Beach, CA 92649-1030
http://www.tcmpub.com

ISBN 978-1-4333-5003-0

© 2013 Teacher Created Materials, Inc.

Table of Contents

Islam

Muhammad

A group of travelers were crossing the desert when a monk saw a cloud over the **caravan**. This was an important sign, thought the monk, so he went to meet the caravan. He met a boy named Muhammad (moh-HAHM-uhd). The monk saw a special sign between Muhammad's shoulders. The monk said the mark meant Muhammad was special.

Muhammad was from Makkah (MAH-kuh), a trading town in ancient Arabia. In the years that followed, he grew up to be a successful trader. He married and had a family. However, as time went on, Muhammad grew weary of his work and even his society. The people around him worshipped many gods and acted in ways he found offensive. He started spending more time alone, thinking in a cave outside of town.

The angel Gabriel visits Muhammad.

Bedouins

Early Life

Muhammad was born in 570. His father had died, so his mother and grandfather raised him. When Muhammad was a baby, they sent him to live among the **Bedouins** (BED-oo-inz) in the desert. People thought that this helped babies grow up healthy, with a pure start. When his mother and grandfather died, young Muhammad was placed in his uncle's care. His uncle taught him how to be a trader.

Makkah or Mecca

Some **Muslims**, or followers of Islam, call their holy city *Makkah* instead of *Mecca* (MEH-kuh). *Mecca* has come to mean "the center of activity" in Western culture. For example, people may call a city a with a lot of shopping malls a "shopping mecca." Some Muslims do not like the name of their holy city used out of context, so they use *Makkah* instead.

In the year 610, an angel named Gabriel appeared before Muhammad in a cave. He brought Muhammad the first of many **revelations**, or words from God. Muhammad was told to serve only one God and that a day of judgment was coming. He was to share these revelations with the world. The boy in the caravan, Muhammad, would become the founder of the religion of **Islam** (is-LAWM).

the Qur'an

The Qur'an

Muhammad shared the revelations with his family and then with others. Muslims think of the revelations as the word of God. They have been recorded in the **Qur'an** (kuh-RAHN), the holy book of Islam. It is said to offer all the guidance a Muslim needs to live a righteous and honorable life.

No Face?

In Islam, picturing Muhammad is wrong. However, some people think his face can be shown as a blank. Others think it is okay to show him with a veil. Covering Muhammad's face is to remind people only to worship God, not humans.

Islamic Beliefs

The revelations were a turning point in Muhammad's life. When they started, he wondered whether he was losing his mind. He questioned what was happening. Later, his beliefs became stronger, and for the next 23 years he instructed the people around him. Some began to see Muhammad as a messenger from God.

Among the most basic beliefs of Islam is the belief in God, his angels, his books, and his messengers. Muslims say that there were thousands of **prophets**, but Muhammad was the final one. Muhammad was chosen to correct what other prophets had said before.

Muhammad rises to heaven.

Another basic belief is that God sits in judgment and people should act accordingly. It is said in Islam that for each person, there is a book. In this book, all the person's deeds are recorded. On the day of judgment, if the book is in the person's right hand, the person can proceed to heaven. If the book is in a person's left hand, that person is destined for a place of suffering. To decide what will happen to someone, God weighs good deeds and bad deeds.

The Five Pillars

Like pillars, or posts, that hold up a roof, the Five Pillars of Worship uphold the Islamic faith. These are the five basic requirements asked of a Muslim. The first is to declare, or say, that there is only one God. The second is to pray daily. The third is to help the needy.

The fourth pillar is to take time to reflect on God and to **fast**, or not eat. Not eating is required only during certain weeks of the year. Muslims typically fast during **Ramadan** (ram-uh-DAHN), the ninth month in the Islamic calendar. They fast from sunrise to sunset to show their love for God.

Time to Pray

In Islam, the times of prayer are set according to where a person lives and the time of year. There are five times to pray: before dawn, at noon, in the afternoon, at sunset, and in the evening. Not all Muslims pray five times a day, but this is considered ideal. People clean themselves beforehand and bow, shoeless, on a special rug or even a newspaper.

Place to Pray

Mosques (mawsks) are places of worship for Muslims. Mosques are built with one wall facing Makkah. These special walls are usually half circles with arches. That way, the right direction to pray can be easily seen.

Muslim men and boys praying

وكـاد يـزع عـن الجـمـال الشـمـس وانشـد

مـا الحـج سـيـر كـت أو بـنـا واد لا جـا ولا لـعـيـنـا جـمـا لا جـمـالا واجـد لا

pilgrims traveling to Makkah

the Ka'ba

The fifth pillar is to make a **pilgrimage** (PIL-gruh-mij), or holy journey, to Makkah. Makkah is not just the trading town where Muhammad grew up; it is also a spiritual center, or symbol, for Islam. In the center of the city of Makkah is a big black cube called the **Ka'ba** (KAH-buh). A cloth decorated with religious verses covers it. When Muslims pray, they face toward Makkah and the cube. If they are inside the Ka'ba, they can pray in any direction.

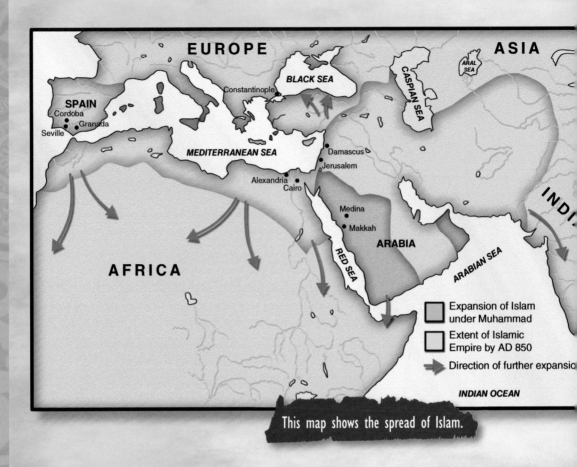

This map shows the spread of Islam.

The Spread of Islam

Muhammad was a man whose story can be told as a **biography**. There are facts about him, such as where he was born and who his family was. However, there is also another Muhammad, a larger one. He lives in the hearts and minds of his followers.

Muslims believe that God judges all people. They must give in to God's will. A Muslim should act in ways that were established by Muhammad. Islam is, on one hand, a religion. It was built on the beliefs of its founder. However, Islam is also a civilization. Muhammad's ideas encouraged groups to band together.

At first, the believers grew as one nation in Arabia. Over time, the number of Islamic nations grew. The borders of the nations under Islam changed. The early period of Islam started with the birth of Muhammad in Arabia. Islam then spread to include parts of Spain, northern Africa, Europe, central Asia, and India. The empire was its largest from 661 to 1258.

In the Clan

Muhammad lived with people who were loyal to their clans. Clans are groups of families. Muhammad wanted people to be loyal to God rather than to their clans. This changed the way power was managed. Under Muhammad, many tribes, or groups of clans, united.

By Name

The clan Muhammad came from was called the Hashim (HA-sheem), for a man by that name. The Hashim guarded the main **shrine** in Makkah. His tribe was called the Quraysh (koo-REYSCH). The Quraysh was the ruling tribe in Makkah.

the Quraysh tribe of the Hashim clan

Muhammad's Death

Muhammad stayed in Makkah, gaining followers, until 622. By then, the leaders of other groups felt threatened and plotted to kill Muhammad. Muhammad and his followers moved to Medina. This move was called the **Hijrah** (HIJ-ruh). At the time of the Hijrah, the Persian Empire was to the east of Arabia. In the north and west was the Eastern Roman Empire. The Muslims pushed back both empires in the years that followed.

In 632, Muhammad returned to Makkah to claim the shrine there. It was being used to worship other gods. Muhammad wanted the shrine to be a place of Muslim worship. After many meetings and agreements with Makkah's leaders and its various groups, Muhammad took control of the city. He led his followers into Makkah. Shortly after that, on June 8, 632, Muhammad died.

Leaders called **caliphs** (KAL-ifs) succeeded Muhammad. The first caliph united tribes in Arabia. The second fought his way into other parts of the Middle East. The third expanded into what is now Libya and Tunisia (too-NEE-zhuh). The fourth moved the capital from Medina to what is now Iraq (ih-RAWK). These first four leaders are called the Rightly Guided Caliphs.

the death of Muhammad

Skilled Politician

Medina representatives were looking for a leader to bring peace to the city. In 622, they met with Muhammad. Muhammad was seen as a skilled politician. He worked to bring the people of Medina together and helped develop a constitution in which the groups that were fighting agreed to give one another rights.

Battle for Minds

The Muslims were often at war with people who wanted to destroy them. Upon returning from an early victorious battle, Muhammad told his people that they must now turn to the "greater **jihad** (ji-HAHD)." This, he told them, is the struggle a person has inside. Rooting out personal flaws, such as greed, is the most important struggle.

the Rightly Guided Caliphs

The Rightly Guided Caliphs

Abu Bakr

These were rough times in Arabia, and the success of the first four caliphs was not a given. At the start, Islam was built around Muhammad. The people swore support to him. He developed their faith and also their government. Islam started as a religious state, where politics and beliefs were in service to each other. When Muhammad died, it was unclear whether things could continue.

There were leaders who stood out, but it was not known if they could manage being both the head of state and also leader of the religion. The first four men who served tried to be both.

the first four Caliphs of Islam

Abu Bakr (ah-BU BA-kuhr) was the first. He was Muhammad's uncle and one of the first people to believe in the revelations. He had helped Muhammad escape from **assassination**. In addition, he was part of the Quraysh, who were still very powerful. Even more significant to some people is that Muhammad was married to Abu Bakr's daughter, Aisha (AH-ee-shah).

Abu Bakr was an older man and was considered wise. He was in many ways an obvious choice to be the first successor. Though some groups did not want Abu Bakr to be the leader, he was still able to keep most of the state of Islam together.

Bringing Stability

Abu Bakr played an important role in early Islam. During a time when people were sad and confused after Muhammad's death, Abu Bakr helped unite Muslims. Under Abu Bakr, Muslims were able to control central Arabia.

Sharia Law

In Islam, **Sharia** (shah-REE-uh) is God's law for all Muslims. *Sharia* means "the path leading to the watering place" because the laws are supposed to help Muslims live a life pleasing to God. The most important idea in Sharia law is to submit yourself completely to God. In some Muslim societies, Sharia law also became the law of the state.

Abu Bakr protects Muhammad from a stoning.

Leading the Way

On his deathbed in 634, Abu Bakr said that Umar (OO-mahr) should rule next. Umar had been Abu Bakr's greatest helper. Under Umar, the state expanded.

When Umar was killed by a slave in 644, Uthman (ooth-MAN) took over. He was part of the Quraysh, who were still powerful. He was also one of Muhammad's original supporters. In addition, he had married one of Muhammad's daughters.

Uthman worked to establish an official version of the Qur'an. Under his command, the state became richer. Power and treasure flowed to Makkah. This all benefited the Quraysh and made people elsewhere hate the rich and powerful in Arabia. In 656, Uthman was assassinated by rebels from Egypt.

Caliph Umar's entrance into Jerusalem

Rebels assassinate Caliph Uthman.

Changed Man

In the beginning, Umar was against Muhammad. However, there is a story that says Umar made a visit to Muhammad's sister's home. She was a follower of Muhammad. When he heard her speak the words of the Qur'an, Umar changed his mind and became a follower of Muhammad.

Umar's Tolerance

Umar was tolerant, or understanding, of Christians and Jews in the areas he ruled. He used the Qur'an to encourage his people to let others live as they wanted to live. Rather than fight people, he tried to win their support.

The council that met when Uthman died gave Muhammad's cousin, Ali, power. However, Ali had powerful enemies. Muhammad's second wife, Aisha, was one of the people who did not like him. Uthman's nephew, the governor of Syria, led armies against him. There was constant fighting. Ali moved the capital to what is now Iraq. He had supporters there. In 661, he was murdered, too.

Looking for Leaders

Taking Sides

When Muhammad died, his people looked for leaders among those who had helped him while he was alive. The most powerful families stepped forward with claims to leadership. It was a dramatic time filled with power struggles. The early caliphs had a hard time controlling such a widespread empire.

The tribes that had banded together under Muhammad had made pledges to him and had promised to serve him. They were released from those promises when Muhammad died. Many of these groups stayed with the new Islamic leadership, but others broke away. Some of the groups had leaders who claimed that they, too, had revelations.

Shi'as fallen in battle

Sufis

The Sufis

The Sufis (SOO-feez) are Muslims who follow a **mystical** path. The Sufis do not focus on individual life. Instead, they give themselves over to something larger. Their worship is surrounded by mystery. The most important knowledge of the Sufis is not written down. They dance as a form of spiritual **meditation**.

War of Apostasy

The revolts after Muhammad's death were called the Wars of **Apostasy** (uh-POS-tuh-see). An apostasy is when someone rejects his or her religion. It can mean many things. It may mean that a person switches religions or mocks the religion. The person denies, in some way, what the religion or God means.

Islam today has many divisions. The two main subgroups are the Sunnis (SUOON-eez) and the Shi'as (SHEE-ahz). Both subgroups agree on the basic principles of Islam. Yet they have political differences. There are also smaller subgroups within each of the larger groups. The majority of Muslims in the world are Sunnis. There are not as many Shi'as as Sunnis. However, the Shi'as hold more power.

Early Shi'as

The first Shi'as were the early Muslims who wanted Ali to be their leader. Ali was Muhammad's cousin. He was married to Fatimah (FAH-tee-mah), who was Muhammad's daughter. She was the only child to outlive him. Fatimah holds a special place in Islam, and many people still pray to her.

Ali was the fourth leader after Muhammad died. The time when he ruled was especially difficult. Ali was murdered soon after taking over. His followers believed that he was cheated out of his place in history.

Some Shi'as believed that Ali and Fatimah's children should be the next leaders of Islam. However, not everyone agreed with this. This caused further divisions among the Shi'as. Some decided that other people were worthy enough to lead Islam and that these leaders just needed to prove themselves.

Today, the leaders of the Shi'as are called *imams* (ih-MAHMZ). They go through a number of steps to rise to the top. The Shi'a imams are considered very special and without sin.

Ali (center) and his sons

بربخ الموتين مرسلته الجنازوقود وإ مالايمن اوقدلاحون رسول عليه السلام

خذمتنه حاضر اولدیدلرحضرته بسالتبیوردیکیم فاطمه ازهرانك
کیلدوکی قماش بوعبينی يلروکو ردلرلما اوتوراریکددماغ اوحمافق

قدنمش

Fatimah receives a gift from the angel Gabriel.

Imams

Some of the differences between Sunnis and Shi'as can be seen in the different ways they view imams. Sunnis saw imams as a caliph. They were political, not religious leaders. But Shi'as viewed imams as sinless religious leaders.

The First Fitna

Ali came to power after Uthman was assassinated. The killers were rebels from another land, but some people suspected that Ali was involved. The first **fitna** (FIT-nuh), or rebellion, began at that time. At its center was Uthman's nephew, Mu'awiya (moo-AH-wee-yuh). He became the first caliph to follow the four Rightly Guided Caliphs.

The Islamic Golden Age

Umayyad warriors

The Umayyad Dynasty

The Umayyad (oo-MAHY-ad) **dynasty** was in power from 661 to 750. After the death of Ali, Mu'awiya came to power. Mu'awiya was an Umayyad, which means he was from Uthman's family.

During their dynasty, the Umayyad had the world's greatest army. Mu'awiya used both **persuasion** and force to take over and expand the empire. This set a pattern for the years to come. Many people who were not Arabs were brought into the faith at this time.

There were 14 Umayyad rulers in all. They greatly expanded the borders of the Islamic state. During their reign, they took over lands across northern Africa. They moved into the Indus Valley. This area is known today as Pakistan (PAK-uh-stan). They also took over areas in what is now Afghanistan (af-GAN-uh-stan), Uzbekistan (ooz-BEK-uh-stan), and Turkmenistan (turk-meh-nuh-STAN). The Umayyad set the stage for what came to be known as the Islamic Golden Age.

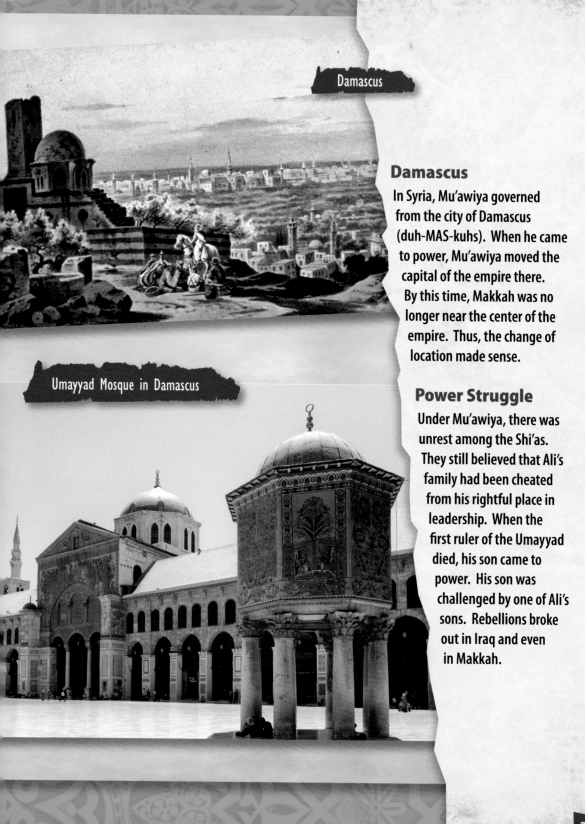

Damascus

Damascus

In Syria, Mu'awiya governed from the city of Damascus (duh-MAS-kuhs). When he came to power, Mu'awiya moved the capital of the empire there. By this time, Makkah was no longer near the center of the empire. Thus, the change of location made sense.

Umayyad Mosque in Damascus

Power Struggle

Under Mu'awiya, there was unrest among the Shi'as. They still believed that Ali's family had been cheated from his rightful place in leadership. When the first ruler of the Umayyad died, his son came to power. His son was challenged by one of Ali's sons. Rebellions broke out in Iraq and even in Makkah.

Abbasid coin

Abbasid mosque

The Abbasid Dynasty

The years from 750 to 1258 were a time of great advancements in the arts and sciences. Trade expanded, and the number of Muslims increased. These were the years of the Abbasid (uh-BAS-id) Dynasty. The Abbasids were descendants of one of Muhammad's uncles. They came to power when fighting broke out again in Persia. The Shi'as fought in the hopes that someone from Ali's family would rule again. However, an Abbasid was placed in charge when the battles ended.

The years under the Abbasids were golden in many ways. Art and culture blossomed. Yet there was plenty of unrest. Shi'as in North Africa rejected the rulers, and slaves revolted as well.

The Shi'as and slaves were not the only challengers. Genghis Khan (GENG-gis kahn) was a fearsome leader from Central Asia. His people were called the Mongols (MONG-guhlz). They wanted to conquer the continent. To do so, they destroyed whatever they found. The Mongol army swooped in from the north. They crushed Baghdad in 1258. This marked the end of the early age of Islam.

The Crusades

Leaders of the Byzantine (BIZ-uhn-teen) Empire wanted to stop the spread of Islam. They asked the leaders of the Catholic Church to help. From 1095 to 1291, the Church sent knights to the Middle East and Western Europe. These missions were called the **Crusades**. Christian soldiers attacked the Muslims. Both religions considered Jerusalem to be a holy city and wanted to control it. The Christians overtook Jerusalem in 1099. It was not until 1187 that Muslims took it back.

Baghdad

The Abbasids built a beautiful new city called Baghdad in what is now Iraq. They made it their capital.

Mongols attack Baghdad.

A New Era

The Gunpowder Empires

When the days of the dynasties ended, Islam entered a new era. A collection of smaller empires with Islamic rulers came into power. These newer states were called the *gunpowder empires*. They were called this because their armies had guns.

The greatest of these empires was the Ottoman Empire. It was based in what is now Turkey. At the height of its power, the Ottoman Empire ruled land around the Black Sea and the Mediterranean (med-uh-tuhr-RAY-nee-uhn) Sea. Their capital was Constantinople (kawn-stan-tuh-NO-puhl), now called Istanbul (is-tahn-BOOL). Their rulers remained in office through 1922.

Suleiman I, sultan of the Ottoman Empire, rides through Constantinople.

the first Mughal emperor

Return of the Caliphate

Many Muslims dream of a "return of the **caliphate**." Caliphate is the Islamic form of government. It means different things to different people, but some Muslims picture one large Islamic nation.

Dar al-Islam

The **dar al-Islam** (dahr ahl-is-LAHM) refers to the land divisions that are under Islamic rule. From the time of the first caliphs to now, the borders have changed dramatically.

The Safavids (sah-FAH-weeds) were a Shi'a group. They ruled over what is now Iran and areas outside it. This newer empire formed as Muslims streamed in from the Abbasid Empire during its breakdown. Its leaders were in power from 1500 to 1722.

The Mughals (MOO-guhlz) rose to power in South Asia. They were not in the majority in the lands that they ruled. Instead, they kept their power by being tolerant. They were successful because they mixed with other people and allowed other forms of worship. The Mughals ruled until the British took over India in 1803. The last emperor was forced out of India in 1858.

Muslim schoolchildren in Kenya

Islam Today

Today, the empires are gone. Yet nearly one in four people practices Islam. In Western civilizations, broad comparisons are often applied to Muslims. The differences between Islamic and Western states are called out, or magnified. Islamic societies tend to be less democratic. Some Muslims, especially women, have fewer freedoms.

These observations are not the whole story of Islam. In the end, perhaps it is most important to learn to see Muslims as individuals. There are Muslims who practice and those who do not. The heart of Islam has many heartbeats.

Today, Islam is the fastest-growing religion in the world. The history of Islam started in the sixth century when a boy named Muhammad was born, and his story is far from over.

Arabic astrolabe

Muslim Contributions

Muslim contributions include the first hospital, which was in Baghdad. Arabs developed algebra and the concept of zero. They also improved the astrolabe, a tool that located planets.

100,000,000

The nations with more than one hundred million Muslims include Bangladesh, India, Indonesia, and Pakistan.

A Muslim girl reads in an Islamic school in Damascus.

Glossary

apostasy—a turning away from one's religion

assassination—to kill an important person by surprise or secret attack

Bedouins—the nomadic tribes of the Arabian, Syrian, and North African deserts

biography—the history of a person's life

caliphate—the area or office ruled by the caliph

caliphs—the Islamic rulers who came after Muhammad

caravan—a group of travelers on a journey through a desert

Crusades—military missions to claim land for Christians in the eleventh, twelfth, and thirteenth centuries

dar al-Islam—the territory ruled by Muslims

dynasty—the lines of rulers that follow from families

fast—to not eat for an extended period of time

fitna—rebellion

Hijrah—the move the first Muslims made from Makkah to Medina

imams—leaders of Islamic religious services

Islam—a religion based on the belief in God and Muhammad as God's prophet

jihad—the struggle to do duty

Ka'ba—the holy shrine in Makkah

meditation—spending time in quiet thinking

Muslims—the people who follow the ways of Islam

mystical—involving experiences of God that are mysterious or not felt by the usual senses

persuasion—the act of winning people over by argument or request

pilgrimage—a journey to a shrine or other sacred place

prophets—people who repeat messages they say are from God or a god

Qur'an—the holy book of Islam

Ramadan—the ninth month of the Islamic year; a month marked by fasting by Muslims

revelations—the communications of divine truth

Sharia—Islamic law; set of laws that teach Muslims how to please God

shrine—a place where someone can pray to a deity

Index

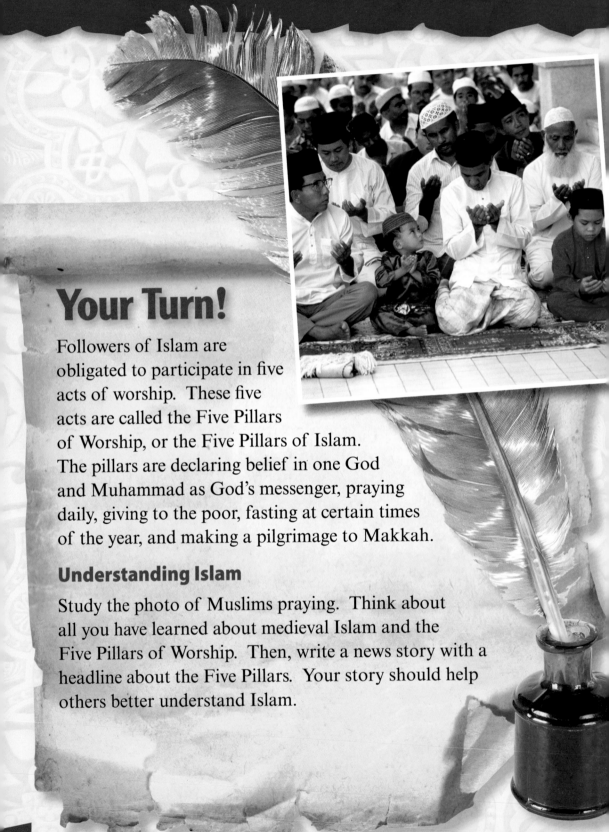

Your Turn!

Followers of Islam are obligated to participate in five acts of worship. These five acts are called the Five Pillars of Worship, or the Five Pillars of Islam. The pillars are declaring belief in one God and Muhammad as God's messenger, praying daily, giving to the poor, fasting at certain times of the year, and making a pilgrimage to Makkah.

Understanding Islam

Study the photo of Muslims praying. Think about all you have learned about medieval Islam and the Five Pillars of Worship. Then, write a news story with a headline about the Five Pillars. Your story should help others better understand Islam.